NIGHT PLOUGHING
and other poems

NIGHT PLOUGHING
and other poems

TULLY POTTER

First Servant Books

NIGHT PLOUGHING and other poems

First Servant Books

CONTENTS

Foreword	page i
Acknowledgements	iv
Preface	v
a piece of bread	1
what giacometti knew	2
poet of st paul's	3
sam beckett of tollund	4
edinburgh	6
1942	8
the walnut tree	10
prisoner of oz	12
the released	13
dear alex	14
to alex	15
the cry of the ha-de-da	16
to alf	18
autumn steps	19
peripatetic	20
daffodils	21
cuckoo!	22
moles	23
potatoes	24
car park	25
caruso of romford market	26
listening to ivor gurney	27
speeding car	28
welcome anaiya	29
welcome laila	30
laila sleeping	31
my pastel child	32
scrutiny	33
making the bed	34
buddleia burst	35
lament for the children	36
the merry child	37
to my daughter	38
intimations	40

the coronation	42
to miriam	44
lines on a beloved brother	45
long distance	46
on the hill	48
autumnal	50
night ploughing	51
wetlands in winter	52
swan quandary	53
clouds of deception	54
ward four	55
the visit	56
x-ray	57
dressing the wound	58
hand dryers	59
hair	60
dispatches from todoland	62
crematorium cat	64
the snake in the net	65
key question	66
the last indignity	67
at twelve today	68
cranmer's vigil	69
for primo levi	70
joanne	72
a happy man	73
the hanged man	74
ukrainian spring	75
address book	76
studland bay	78
girl	79
the fiddler's dream	80
in the square	82
three wise monkeys	83
this is the verse	84
the great writer	85
two haiku	86
nocturnal	87

First Serva

Publisher of

Poetry, Art, Local Histo

Tel & Fax: 81+(0)4-7137-7152   E-Mail: firstservant@gm

To Whom It May Concern:

A Request to Review the followir

NIGHT PLOUGHING

by TULLY POTTER

A landmark collection of over
selected poems.

This is his first collection sinc

With compliments

First
Servant
Books

ant Books

Specialized Books

ory, Fiction, Biography & Memoirs

ail.com   Website: www.firstservantbooks.jp

g book:

nd other poems

eventy of Tully Potter's new and

he Emigrant (1975)

FOREWORD

Tully Potter is highly respected for his writings on music. Less widely well known at the present time, perhaps, are his poetical works. His last major collection, *The Emigrant, and Other Poems,* was published almost fifty years ago, in 1975, and since then only a handful of his poems have appeared in publications. In those long ago years, as fellow poets we had quite a number of exchanges and were very much on the same wave-length, but we never had the chance to meet face to face until five years ago (September, 2018), when we met at The King's Head, Sevenoaks, where he kindly treated us to lunch – in spite of the fact, as his good wife Jill had recently reminded him, I had once very unjustly accused him of plagiarizing my poetry! That just shows how closely we saw and still see eye to eye on things poetical. Earlier that year he had sent me most of the poems that appear in this book, and once again I realized that Tully, as I wrote in my diary, is "a poet after my own heart. He really 'does things' with language, uses words in new ways, and his verse is full of 'music' and sound." This is, as I wrote to him, "what all true poets, scops. shapers, makers, word-smiths, do, and what very few people writing poetry nowadays do... But yours: yours sing out, loud and clear and cry 'These are real poems!'. Ted Hughes (in his earlier poems) and Dylan Thomas have this extraordinary facility with words... Again and again in these poems of yours I come across memorable sentences and phrases: 'your hands dangle beyond fondling', 'it is you/who hurt in all these houses', 'to spend their last gasps on magnificence', 'another sucks your ticket in/without grace', 'and sometimes the phoenix flutters/from the ashes of a better bird'."

Not only because of their highly original usage of words, Potter's poems also have an immediacy that instantly attracts the reader. Their deceptive simplicity of expression gives them a magical quality which delights on first encounter, and then invites deeper examination, which is always rewarding. His poems have the rare ability

i

to sparkle brightly on the surface while shining with a deeper luminescence like the clear, fresh water at the bottom of a well.

This collection covers an enormous canvas. The range of subjects is extraordinary. He takes us through woodland ways to the very pith of nature, and guides us through the joys of companionship to the aching losses of good friends. He gazes upon the very young with delight as they discover the world, yet death is a constant dark presence lurking in the background and sometimes at the very front of the stage. Tully Potter strides with ease through the galleries of tragedy, comedy, romance and cool intellect. He is both critic and admirer. The serious walks hand in hand with the ridiculous. Potter is a poet of all colours. He paints with words; his landscapes are full of sound. In *night ploughing*, the tractor's 'gruff engine quarrels with the still air' and 'october stalks across our graves'.

Years ago, when I first encountered Potter's refusal to use capital letters in his poems, I thought this rather eccentric and gimmicky, or just an overt imitation of the style of the American poet e. e. cummimgs, who made this style of writing popular, and from whom, Tully admits, "I caught the lower-case bug." But more recently, he made his reasons for doing this more clear to me. "Way back in 1975," he writes, "we used the general Poetry One style: putting the title of each poem in bold italic... It seems a more elegant way of doing things, seeing that I like to write in lower case. Is this just an affectation? I think not. It's a sincere desire to make all the words the same, so that they will stand out by their inherent importance, rather than some convention." I find this convincing.

I feel greatly honoured and privileged to have this opportunity to write a Foreword, and to have a part in the readying of this rare collection for the wide world.

Gavin Bantock
July, 2023

To two great editors,
Derek Parker
and the late Lionel Abrahams,
who were the first
to see merit in my poetry
and publish it

ACKNOWLEDGEMENTS

A Piece of Bread was published in *Samphire, Vol. 3 No. 7,* Summer 1980; and read on BBC2 Television by Martin Jarvis.

To Alf was published in *Poet: An International Monthly, Vol. 7 No. 6,* August 1966.

Prisoner of Oz was published in *Weyfarers,* Guildford Poets Press, No. 37, August 1983.

Cuckoo! & *Moles* were published in *Ver Poets Voices No. 8.*

My Pastel Child was published in *Gateway No. 19,* December 1979; and republished [with misprint] in *Samphire Vol. 3 No. 8,* Spring 1981.

Buddleia was published in *Weyfarers, Guildford Poets Press, No. 37,* August 1983.

On The Hill was published in *From the City to the Saltings: Poems from Essex,* 2013.

Girl was published in *Samphire 15,* April 1972.

Joanne was published in *Outposts Poetry Quarterly, No. 135,* Winter 1982.

Front cover illustration:
Resident
No. 41 of Forty One Approaches to a View,
Paper, 14x21cm, Indian Ink
and a single dipping nib (round Leonardt, 6)
CUILLIN BANTOCK, 2022

Back cover illustration:
Tully Potter: A Caricature
HARO HODSON, 1984

PREFACE

Many of these poems are relatively recent and most are unpublished. Nine have previously appeared in books or magazines. One was read on BBC-2 Television.

I would like to express fervent thanks to Gavin Bantock, for all his encouragement and the work he has undertaken in bringing this book to fruition, and to Stephen Miller, for his unstinting help and constructive criticism over the years.

Their friendship, the love of my family and the comradeship of many other writers - notably the late Alex Smith, who is remembered in three of the poems - have been constant sources of energy, inspiration and stimulation for me.

Tully Potter
July, 2023

a piece of bread

rembrandt had eyes for such as this:
the antique patina of crust,
pitted and polished as if by use,
the veins, caves and runnels of crumb

in what strange ways you can gaze at it!
from the top, crustwards, bald and bumpy;
or below, relishing those intimate curves
where the loaf hunched itself against the heat;
then the sides, each a unique frieze
concealing its network of capillaries

you can pinch, knead, roll it in your palm
until its puffed pomp is dough again,
though now with no hope of resurrection;
you can break it and bomb it
bit by bit, convoyed by crumbs,
into thick soup – watching as each soaks,
lurches, resigns and sponges down
to lurk just below the surface

you can bless it as a holiness,
a bringer of birds

or you can grab it, without grace,
in both hands and wolf it back
with scarcely a taste,
more the sensation of the throat
filled first, then the stomach,
the sweet stealing of unused juices;
any crumbs dispersed
can be ferreted from coat folds or beard
and absorbed, intently,
your eyes quite ignorant of rembrandt

what giacometti knew

what giacometti knew
was the essence of a man,
the marrying of form and motion
that make a woman:
the heartstopping glimpse
of loved one or enemy
out of the corner of the eye

how our instincts fashion
a maquette of the person,
a flicker, as in a flickbook,
of their being:
the amalgam of hair
and movement and attitude
flashing their physical emanation
before they are fully seen

the sick devastation
or deep relief
when the reality turns out
to be someone else entirely

all this, giacometti knew

poet of st paul's

the frail eggshell of his head
moves below domes, towers and battlements
but contains them

bell-claps fall clanging about his ears,
words drift down in ticker-tape torrents
and still he holds to his road

his mind, hovering, poised on china bones
light as shells, rounded and fertile,
loves and enfolds all

the great dome cracks, its gold cross
over-topples and drops almost at his feet,
the towers tumble, the debris showers down
yet not a frown ruffles his fragile forehead

a cruel crane crunches through the walls,
the very brains of st paul's spatter and spill
and in the dust the poet walks,
his delicate ho-chi-minh head
encompassing ruin and renewal

sam beckett of tollund

freshly delved out, you arrived,
walking timeless to the table,
you sat and thought
without talking
while we talked unthinking

your cheeks bore the stigmata
of many centuries of submersion
or subterranean laughter,
the skin taut and tough,
the lines hacked
out of the fibrous heart of the peat,
the hair dry-blown back as grey grass,
the sea-sky eyes fathomless

round your un-noosed neck
no restraint
but you too, we fancied,
had torn your tether loose:
disinterred, more alive than dead,
you were more dead than half-alive,
making us laugh at death

but then, you always creased us
with your athlete's face
and, for all we knew, aesthete's foot,
ascetic if not aseptic sam
with your weathered air
of surprise
at your own surmise

how would they bury you at last?
in praise?
or was the grave your cradle?
you, with your outgoing containment,
your spare abundance

you blessed us with a curse (a hearse!
my kingdom for a hearse!)
and weeks, years, centuries
after you forgave time,
we stayed blest

edinburgh

all of a piece, the castle and the old town
set off one another's firmness,
each house
a frock-coated, bristle-whiskered elder
comprehending
the stern-worded sermon in stone
descending from above

yet there is beauty
in their rolling periods
and knox-knocking auguries of fire;
there is grandeur
in these high-ceilinged, high-principled rooms,
the pride of the unendingly unbending

*

auld reekie has had me in her grasp
since i first, as a grown man,
drove into her stony embrace

a city of sensible men
and warm women – or so they say;
a changeable town
for all her teeming seeming substance;
a jekyll and a hyde,
the flow of reason
checked by the logic of disapproval

*

drunk with words,
the poet in the pew
clenches numbing buttocks
and awaits the wrath to come

excess, yes, is frowned on
but fine verbiage is all we have
to stem the sabbatarian tone

*

city of my birth,
why do you blow rain into my face?
do you accuse me
of absence,
of not keeping the faith?

we scots, i am telling you,
have our own way of staying true
and fair weather has no part in it

1942

as i was beginning
what end was being shaped for you?

what maw,
what inverse, perverted womb
gaped for you?
could i, slapped suddenly into crying,
be delivered free of guilt?

my children,
confreres in bone, in flesh,
see, the bodies are without number,
the waning eyes,
the unshrieking throats
and the quiet that is beyond weeping

o fathers, mothers, you
who are all worlds and all moments,
the obscene apathy of time is in a face
hanging down, past martyrdom

this grief, my brothers,
transcends emotion or degradation,
your eyes are void even of innocence,
your minds
beyond the reach of philosophy

if you had smiled, my sisters,
your mouths would have made arches
for the entrances of the generations
but your hands dangle beyond fondling,
they pile the bodies on the bodies,
eye on eye, tooth on tooth

o my millions,
my millions upon millions
of imperfectly perfect persons

o stigmata, mouthing like lips,
o sacred scars,
o blessed blemishes, true relics
of the last silent sadness

my comrades,
your song is witness to its own sorrow,
your bodies are beyond bleeding
and your eyes beyond tears

the walnut tree

it was there when we moved in,
a great bush of a thing on a long trunk,
with suggestive scars
where lower branches had been lopped

its bark was abrasive, its waxy leaves
were late to unfurl each spring,
as if the tree
were reluctant to show its hand too soon

one branch sportingly supported a swing;
the trunk oozed black
when i hammered in a bracket
for a feeder the birds would never use

nor did we gain many walnuts:
guarded by black-bleeding blankets,
they caused more strife to dry
than they were worth; and each year
scrumping squirrels scampered up
into the confused canopy
to squirrel down gingerly,
their scrotal mouths full of two nuts

and then the tree shed its leaves
which quilted lawn and flowerbeds

on the night of the big storm
i saw in the early hours
how our walnut tree
was twisted over like a twig;
and in the morning
the trunk had shifted inches
in the soft autumn ground

but still it stood,
ungainly, defying the tree surgeon
to shape its lollipop top

the folk who bought our house
had it brought down, saying
it made the place too dark

strange ... for me its presence
was a source of light

prisoner of oz

you know him, the tin woodman,
though you may not laugh
– he may not threaten
even your sense of humour

you know his axe is tinny
and would buckle on wood,
his armour could not fend off a fist;
the grin is welded on to his face,
hardly enough brainwaves bound
around his helmet of a head
to make him a mad axeman

you see him striding
along his clumsy pathways
and you assume
he must have some refuge,
a tin-can cabin
where he brews metallic tea

you never greet him
or ask him the way
though you think of him as a friend;
his own trees, trailing their leaves,
cannot console his cold shoulders,
the voles avoid his crashing feet

perhaps the lightning would love him
but the rain would raise rust

he must have a heart, you feel,
else how could he keep going?
if he has lusts, appetites,
a hollowness hides them

the released

you soon learn
not to ask a question,
not even 'how are you?'

a look, even of love,
can disturb scar tissue

hands
nervily exploring
the lack of shackles
are not yet ready to grasp yours

eyes
are all too ready
to slide off-beam

to see the torturer's face
reflected in a friend's gaze
is in itself
a kind of torture

14

dear alex

as hairlines recede, so do recollections ebb:
i no longer recall
when we first met, or where

what i do know of, is the space
in the deepest recesses of my awareness
that has long been yours

i cannot calculate comradeship,
the figures do not conjugate:
the physical figure, yes,
the burly frame,
the loud, volcanic mirth,
the shining features,
the bustling enthusiasm

the talk i can remember,
of poems, poets and the strange interplay
between them;
the music i easily recreate

the 'something other' eludes me

old friend,
these words will not assuage pain
but they are driven into existence
by urgings
i can only name as love

to alex

the abrupt, eruptive laugh,
the more than beaming, almost gleaming face,
the limitless grin

the loving handling of book or disc,
the longing to explain
miles, bird, mingus, coltrane,
the sheathed vinyl
reverently returned to its shelf

johnson's richness,
eliot's or tomlinson's spareness,
the different madnesses of stevens or lowell
spoke to you
as you drank their phrases down
and, having read,
found places for them

for you the book was a sacrament,
the sonnet a psalm

the hands that paid their tribute to poetry
also pressed fellowship into our hands;
your voice honoured us
with its exuberance,
even as it weakened

rest easy, old friend

the cry of the ha-de-da

the cry of the ha-de-da,
sigh of a purgatoried soul,
calls to me from the no-person's-land
between prosaic earth and heaven

how shall we mourn those who are gone,
it asks, how remember them?
when those we counted on
to survive us
have crept out, what threnodies?
what tocsins?

alex, in the fraught early hours
i make a note to tell you
of another poet found:
like the red stretches of australia
myriad scribes who felt and suffered
wait to be discovered

but i am old now;
how can i push back the frontiers
without you
at the other end of a phone?

those afternoons of repartee
return to me,
your rubicund face glowing
at each palpable hit

hill i never could abide, or tomlinson,
but i never told you
or mentioned that the same anecdote,
prompted by the identical verse,
was well worn to me

now i feel i could come clean
but you
are a number unobtainable,
your voice is like the cry of a bird
in the insubstantial air

to alf

i hear myself speaking of spring flowers
to you, who will not see another spring:
naming snowdrop, crocus, primrose
will not make the season come sooner
but we may spin
a net, through which
the wet and weariness of winter
will be more dimly seen

the wind wails
and pins the raindrops to the window
but in here is warmth
amid the thoughts of not-quite-gone;
as we wait to walk away from you
we luxuriate
in not thinking of next week

when daffodil shoots show
like fingers of the dead,
the birds will blather
in blithe ignorance of your passing
but we shall know

last night foxes were barking,
readying themselves
for the renewal to come;
and yet today
a bird table skittled by the wind
mocked us in the garden

against your pillows of feathers
you rest,
thin and beaky as a fledgling
and not yet free to fly

autumn steps

a month until the shortest day
and the year gropes to its close
like a gassed and blinded soldier

even the trees
have been spilling their leaves
and voting for death

browned around my shoes,
lumping underfoot,
their cast-offs
cushion my steps

yes, the trees are tramp-ragged
but their rags
have a richness
not seen in their full dress

they have become jesters
or cavaliers,
vibrant in adversity

how brave it is
that on the point of dying
for another season,
they choose
to spend their last gasps
on magnificence

peripatetic

i take the same walk every day,
the sameness underlines the differences,
the new or known people greeted,
the dogs
with their own dogged agendas

birdsong does not deflect me,
it quickens my steps

the bitter east wind reminds me of li po;
i inwardly salute all wanderers
and my feet carry my thoughts
back to the peripatetics

i have no pat philosophy for today
but the regular rhythm of the trudge:
the click of my stick,
should allow my brain to balloon free

i am too tied to the earth
and at the same time too vaporous;
the thoughts i ought to be having
cannot moor themselves,
they splinter
and spin off into irrelevance

and yet ... i am content

daffodils

shrill trumpets,
elegant as telephones
and poised
to broadcast or receive;
random guardlights
gangling
over spiky palisades

unpaid informers,
lissome listeners,
the merest breath
setting them sniding

ageing gossips
wrinkling
into bitter,
still-blonde harridans

mocking even death,
the lying-in-state
becoming a lying-in;
every last one
assured
of a two-faced renaissance

cuckoo!

cuckoos are better heard than seen
yet the cry,
half music, half mocking,
invites discovery

so we tracked him,
fooled by the rule
that no matter how close you go,
the bird is always further

now we had him circled;
though his ageless, timeless chime
surrounded us

obsessed by our quest,
we trampled bluebells
more lovely than any cuckoo
and barely knew our crime

so that when our child cried
and we heard the flurry of the bird,
our sighs embraced relief

a cuckoo missed
is a myth still to be known
and, however primped his plumage,
merely brown

moles

brown mounds on skin or lawn,
oases for the eye,
loving smudgers of smoothness,
pride prickers,
under-shovellers of the slick,
the soft sheen

o imperfectionists!

come up often
from your tunnels of fun,
erect your tufts,
your tuffets, tussocks or divots,
divert us from all smugness

fix our eyes upon the fallible,
the lovelier
for being rougher

blemish the trim, the prim,
the creamy or too graciously green,
bring us down to brown!

potatoes

go in for a testicular type of lurking

unmasked, shaken free
of the obstinate earth
how smooth and plain they seem

tortured with boiling
they betray nothing
but yield to teeth
with untrustworthy resistance

i hear them called humble
and yet
their refusal to yield a taste
has a kind of arrogance

car park

with a nose like a bent button,
celebratory cheeks,
the old geezer was the sort
you might have thought
had invented cheerfulness

quite the wrong generation
for 'have a nice day'
but as he took your ticket,
or fumbled for change
in an all too fallible way,
deflecting your apology
with a 'that's okay, guv',
he put a fine flourish into
'mind how you go'

some days he saluted
in a half-remembered hangover
of smarter manoeuvres

did he or his ramshackle booth
disintegrate first?

as you enter now
a machine puts its tongue out at you
and as you leave,
another sucks your ticket in
without grace

caruso of romford market

amid the medley of pedlars,
cabbage, clothes and crockery sellers
and importunate, mendicant marketfolk
his cry resounded:
'arf a crown yer ironin'-board covers,
all standard size!

compact and focused
like the tenors of legend,
he hung his wares over one arm
while the other gestured operatically

always at the arcade entrance,
his back straight,
his chin down,
his head at just the right angle to project,
his well-worn face almost apoplectic:
a megaphone of a man,
the caruso of cryers

i think he disappeared
before what we all called d-day,
at least i hope he did
– the peasant poetry of such a cry
would never have survived
being decimalised

listening to ivor gurney

a voice draws words
athwart the piano's prelude
and i think of severn,
his river,
mud-brown, overswollen,
and the swoop of blue
defining
a kingfisher

on a branch afterwards
the bird seemed just as jewelled
but in a quandary,
between purposes, listless,
like poor gurney
wrestling with notes and words
mangled by the maelstrom

and yet our journey
had its justifying:
a bird found silver
and we knew that emphatic flash
when a sliver of sky
inspired the umber flood

speeding car

the headlights find out the dark,
we move, separate yet part of life,
through the world; the quiet tyres
scarcely know our movement

we are encased in our own world,
other planets pass us and are gone;
it is a clash of stars if we collide
(we should have to leave our cocoons
to acknowledge others like us,
review our smashed worlds)
– better not to meet

we are safe spacemen, spinning;
the dark
is a stocking on the face,
we are contorted in space,
capsuled, separate,
free-falling

(like a headlight on a pole
i explore my openings
as i hurtle out of world;
i spin within myself,
searching myself)

all things are constant
speeding in the darkness

welcome anaiya

surveillance caught you for us,
in your undersea cavern:
we saw you hover,
keeping your counsel,
stoking your mysterious strength;
we heard your heartbeat
counting off the hours

week by week
we watched with trepidation
for your fearful coming;
and then
your head was crowned
and you were there,
as if you had always been
our queen
but had not been fully seen

decanted into the light
you seemed strangely aged,
your roar
more of distress than anger,
your fingers ill-used to eloquence

we found our hearts giving way

all-knowing you may be
but your old-woman look
promises to become young;
there will be time
for love, play and sadness,
for flirting, flighting, even fighting

let the years lie in wait:
for the present, wise child,
you can afford
to pick them off one by one

welcome laila

nine months you lurked
unseen, except by machines:
building up
your domed beaver lodge
where you swam, fed
and, for all we knew,
frolicked

rumours reached us
of reckless moves,
nocturnal foot games,
but you
kept your counsel

now that you have moled out
into our surface world,
you still curl up
to hibernate

your eyes regard us
guardedly
from a still wrinkled face,
you keep your voice
for emergencies

but something
in the way you fit
into our arms
tells us
you are in command

laila sleeping

dormouse-curled,
mazed in your mythic world,
what will you make
of our kingdom of the awake?

i see your dream-time break
like a newly skincast snake
or a chrysalis unfurled,
iridescent, pearled

my pastel child

my pastel child
is powdered by sleep
in pinks and creams
and the most delicate dustings
of blue

translucent lashes
fringe her silk-sashed eyes,
the blonde-brown curls
hug her seashell head
more caressingly
than the crook of my arm

only the clock menaces our peace,
meting out her sleep
and my stewardship

scrutiny

child,
your depth-dark eyes
fix on us
as if you know all our past

your age-old gaze
tracks us unflinchingly
but, silent,
you withhold judgment

you do not accuse
though we are almost ready
to blurt out our sins

then, as time passes,
you become younger:
you smile at last
and we
can forgive ourselves

making the bed

after the bending, the battering and bolting,
after the bruising,
the muscling-in of screws,
the scrutinising and perusing of blueprints,
behold a bed!

i watch you mount the steps
to your present concept of heaven,
i dream of dreams
you will dream there

the old blue bed
(not so old – it matched your eyes
and once excited you)
sets out on its own voyage
into exile

so we have made our ark
and all the animals on the wallpaper
will march

i cannot say what waves will wash you
on your way
today,
much less tomorrow
(dove of rescue, flood of sorrow)
– i have no blueprint for your growing
waking or sleeping

it is far easier to build a bed
(or a life-raft)
than to lie on it...

buddleia burst

feeding butterflies flood the buddleia
with eyes – bleary blazing
and alien
until my own sight sorts each insect
out of camouflage

tentatively eager,
they exude a tremulous tranquillity
all too fragile
– the shrub will shrug them off
in fewer hours than its flowers

my child chuckles
and moves to touch a rouged wing
– i must restrain her
though i fear to brush the bloom
from her cheek

i tell myself
a daughter's blue brilliant eye
and veined porcelain
must last for longer than a day

lament for the children

pibrochs are fit for heroes, not for those
who, having borne our hopes,
fade before us

they merit a softer piping

it is the possibilities we mourn,
the unforeseen might-have-beens,
not the silly dreams of queens and kings
but more down-to-earth pangs

the love implicit
in the laying-out of breakfast,
in meeting-greetings after school,
the carrying on our shoulders
of something light and lithe and live,
blood of our blood, bone of bone

we think those hands too small
to bear lines of death as well as life

in the pathetic, forever fixed pictures
peering from screen or front page
we sense long lacerations of everyday loss

in eyes that follow us
as we leave the children's ward
(we who can come and go as we please)
we see not requiems or public manifestations
but worn toys, thrown down,
untidy in an empty room

the merry child

the smile asks nothing

it wells up
from the elfin depths
of her nine-months-old being,
rippling like an airwave
of pure joy

it promises nothing
but unconditional love

to my daughter

FOR RACHEL

it is your hand i remember,
warm and soft and small,
a child's hand
sliding confidingly into mine
as we wait at the crossing
for the 'green man'

i still feel it there sometimes,
infinitesimally tiny
when enveloped by my vast paw,
not cloying or clinging,
a token of total trust

a daughter's hand is not a lover's
or a wife's or even
somewhere between the two:
it is a strange and yet a loving thing
to be tight warmed and kept in faith
for a new lease of living

often i have wished your path
were as plain,
as brightly lit and laid out
as that road of long ago:
there is no man in green to send for,
no miracle machine
i can call in aid
if you trip and fall

and now, as i hand you to another,
i know my care is shared
but not halved

i only trust that, when i stumble in my turn
into childhood,
your hand, still younger but now firmer,
will steady me
as i cross

intimations

if this should be your last afternoon
let the land fall away from you
in layers
like the lost levels of your life;
let the children's voices waft up to you
but let the past condone its own

let the birds attend to you
if they can hear the swansong of your mind;
allow the trees to close in on you

in these last hours
being is all,
the honest fixing of your eyes
on no horizon;
folk in the valley
are not far projections of yourself
but their own entities;
now is when you must let them go
and they must leave you be

the air is balanced
between breeze and breath;
you glimpse the scene through green
the summer through the filter of spring,
an autumn implicit in the leaf's outline;
to count the growth-rings of your being
would be to kill its cause

it must be enough
to let the ground sink
and with it, all children who call;
once you would have held it up
and groaned under its load
but now the earth can moan as it will;

no need to think of wounding it
with a gash long enough for you
– there will be time and takers for that,
as for all things that come after
this last afternoon

the coronation

TO MIRIAM

i did not see your head crowned

i was confined to the outer circle,
condemned to look, nonplussed,
at the plain smooth walls
of some corridor

as i saw more doctors arrive
like whitecoated cavalry,
i was not thinking of you,
i had no inkling of you
except an unseen footkicking
football of a bulge
without even a sex

it was your mother in my thoughts
in those minutes of no-man's-time:
what mysteries
were they practising on her?
what honings of the knife?

and then they brought you,
huddled in the almost anonymity
of a blanket,
aged in the womb, a strange vintage
come to make our hearts drunk
all over again

i saw you grow
younger and then older
in the way of your kind

i saw you flower

and now, daughter,
when i think i see
motherhood in your eyes
i wonder what, in your own fair time,
you will bring to the crowning

to miriam

we hate to see our children walk away;
we hold our image of them
every way we can,
in sight, in mind, we say

through that walk that takes them from us
they change and grow,
then dwindle into distance,
presenting different backs to us
from those we think we know

so now, as i strain after
your still retreating form, daughter,
and see you choose a partner's hand,
i know our link has somehow become less
yet also know
that i must wave you on
and as i see you go,
raise my own hand not to grasp
or to restrain
but bless

lines on a beloved brother

TIM POTTER 1938-2020

a quiet man:
while we were chattering,
you would bide your time
until you found worthwhile words

a gentle man
but firm with it,
a verbal version
of your handshake

a brace of brilliant eyes
that saw through all bluffs
and blathers

a kind man,
slow to anger,
truly terrible in wrath

a pipe smoker,
philosophical between puffs

a fine voice
in song or speech,
a fine-tuned humour

in all, a big man,
brother, father, friend
and lover

now you have slipped
into a deeper quietness,
you leave a space
it will take a real man to fill

long distance

you sounded, as i strove to construct you
from pulsations,
as if you were recalling yourself
by a weary but still fierce effort of will

the gulf between us
was greater when told by distance
but no deeper

your age did not like to speak its mind
and i ... i always had more in me
of you
than i could bear to see

on that final day, too,
your voice, coming
as from a long way off
before it even reached the receiver,
was recognisably yours;
you were your self still,
even on the threshold

at what point, precisely,
did you cease to be your self,
that amalgam of voice and choice
which was indubitably you,
and somehow become someone else's words
bringing bad news?

as if a voice broke in
saying that all the lines were down,
an uninvolved, impersonal tone

was there a click
as you closed your colloquy with life?

or was it imperceptible
even to you?

call me from where you are:
i am ready to receive
but the signals crackle and are confused
and when i make them out,
i find my own words echoing on the line

it is my voice vibrating,
my own heart that pounds,
drowning you out

how sad
and in this age of over-honesty
how strange
that it is easier to speak
now you are silent

on the hill

the oaks tell us it is autumn:
the dwindling days
shade their ingeniously jigsawed leaves
through colours which recall your face,
honest browns, reds and golds
of an openhearted, openhanded season

a time when you were most at ease,
the wheat razed, the hay trussed,
acres tilled and seeded
and the glow in your pipe's bowl
steady, lengthening into winter;
your features carved in hard wood
and seemingly impervious to years

when we spoke under the great oaks
marking out your meadows,
i thought you stood stout as they,
nutted and rutted by weather,
your ancient essex accent
less fallible than your farm fields
or the barns that crumbled round

now the oaks flare in their places
but you are felled,
laid up on oaken trestles
as a sign to family, foes, friends;
oak bears them up, too, in stiff pews
and at the prayer stall your father made
the rector mouths

outside on the gaping grave
two well-worn oak staves wait
to take your strain
before the last lowering;

against a heeling headstone
the homely implements lean

these you would have known,
would have hefted in your hard hands
with pleasure:
used and soil-stained
and proper to their task
like the tools that served you

i see you slap the well-shaped sides
of your niche, adjudging a job done
by one of your own kind:
the tapered, sinister outline
well punched into the hillside,
the cut earth
brown and beaten as your face

only the box itself seems too new,
too polished and parlour-bright,
bringing its air of smartness,
its corner-sharpness
to your well-rounded wake

no matter: it will not contain you;
the hill will take you to herself
and turn you, impermeable as ever
toward the weather

autumnal

brown, green, gold, green
– the colours of the scene ease the eye;
autumn has not yet confounded them

a lone tractor in alien red
is an insect irritating to soil and to serenity;
the farmer, known even from this far,
bows ageing at the wheel,
weathered face over green coat, brown trousers;
in the furled earth
a grounded crowd of gulls flounders

the eye, sweeping up and over the blind sky,
finds further furrows:
a plane traverses, pulling out its white plumes
to halve the blue pool

no figure there, familiar to the view,
the plane a mere badge against a uniform coat,
the man careering in it
immaterial to the issues of autumn:
a silver ghost of movement, ploughing grooves
which already some drunk ariel is erasing

down here the field is rich with brown cleavage
– it is here the birds hanker,
not after the ploughboy of the sky

the eye too will tire
of all that blatant blue,
those vivid cloud veils and vapour trails;
the shades of brown and green and in-between
salve the autumnal soul

night ploughing

the moon draws clouds across her face
to see those rogue earthbound moons
profane the sacred soil

tracking, backing and retracking,
the tractor quarters the field

its questing lights
reverse the natural order of things,
scything through the night
even as its six bright blades bite,
folding over the dark loam
into yet more blackness

its gruff engine quarrels with the still air,
quieting the querulous tawny owl,
scaring foxes, shrews, badgers
and all vestiges of life

october stalks across our graves
with a familiar shiver

must death really descend
and cast his felt cloak over the lost land
before the spring can surprise us?

wetlands in winter

on the inscrutable water
the ducks inscribe their wakes;
impelled
by some inner duck imperative
they strike out purposefully
or fly athwart the waterscape

a swan stands on one leg,
impervious to the incongruity
of its pavlova yoga pose;
two geese gabble,
stretching out provocative necks

here flooding, inimical to man,
is the wader's ecstasy

all nature moves
to a more fluid impetus
than politics or our other passions,
each duck as intent on finding food
as any peasant

the dry tall reeds and grasses
hide an infinite wariness:
bitterns, water rails
heard but not seen,
are promises as unfulfilled
as any human preoccupation

swan quandary

the swans move, immutably mute,
enigmatic, balletic,
eternally emblematic:
their very heads and necks
are question marks

the pen a model of motion, gliding
innocent as a nun,
but with one foot
inelegantly held up

the cob serene now,
with a mellow mindfulness,
quite banishing the scene of yesterday
when he was thrashing, flailing
from end to end
of a suddenly small-seeming lake:
innate power, pent-up fury unleashed,
a water-borne tide of terror
in feathers;
a beast of a bird
unconcerned about making a scene
or attracting admiration

today they are at one
with one another
and us wary watchers,
content to leave coots,
geese, moorhens, ill-spoken ducks
and the like
all floundering in their wake

clouds of deception

clouds give promise of permanence,
pale structures
of snow or spun ice,
fancifully stacked steps and towers,
not so much castles in the air
as staircases i can never ascend
to a heaven i shall never inhabit

the sky, meanwhile,
as it always was when i was a child,
is a great blue dome,
unviolated by astronauts
and their crude penetrations

i should be keeping my thoughts
on the day's tasks,
the knitting of words,
but my mind sideslips into reverie
as my eyes size up the clouds

do they aggrandise themselves,
rising up
in their folds and follies,
like our aspirations?

i am told the kingfisher's blue
is as illusory as the sky,
a sleight-of-hand of the light;
still, in my childish way,
i persist in fixing my faith
on such delights of transience

ward four

they are drawing the curtains for you,
mr english, dramatically
cutting you off from us
with a cloth corridor
down which your bed can glide
in silence
– the quiet which was denied you
by your own rasping breath
and hourly sorties of nurses
to lift you, turn you
and move you
still no further away
from death

i waved to you one morning
across the chasm of your gasping mouth,
until our eyes collided
and from your side
an answering arthurian hand rose;
i would have reached to grasp it
before it sank
back into the lake-like limpidity
of the dying;
but i told myself
you would survive
to be embarrassed

they draw the curtains every evening,
mr english;
but for one daytime instant
you have torn the cloister of cloth
to make your night
our night

the visit

breaking the armed neutrality
of health squaring up to sickness,
i sit on the bed: the crisp coverlet
crinkles, its rucks radiating
as if in search of a connection

you rest upright, your mind wriggling
even as your talk maintains poise;
you evoke an insect, still outwardly itself
but sucked almost dry of life,
each faint buzz merely a confirmation
of the web's embrace

our words will never wing between us
as they once did:
only a small-talker could say
you look your old self;
too many strings,
all sticky with fear or guilt,
stretch around us to strangle discourse

even wrinkles in the bedspread
seem calculated – spontaneity
would be out of place here,
where straight lines fashion square holes
for lopsided pegs like you

i know that when i leave
and we exchange our prepared statements,
your knee flexing under the counterpane
will expunge my creases,
even as you wipe your face clear of lines
ready for the next friend

x-ray

laid on my side,
hand on hand, leg on leg,
i represent
a strange antique burial

bent into the foetal fantasy
of my beginning,
i lack only the artefacts of brass,
the pots and weapons
that should attend my end

i am defenceless
against prurient rays:
laid out for archaeology,
so much meat or bone
or liquor
for the operator to prod,
push or pat
before a screen conceals her

i am revealing
those things i shudder to know
should be within me, the aspects
i loathe to contemplate

it is my history in reverse, rehearsing
for that moment
five days, weeks, years away
when i shall lie like this
without a care

dressing the wound

the firm, probing assault,
the scissoring of soiled bandage,
the tender
but still uneasy peeling,
the laying bare

the washing
– something sacramental in that –
the dabbing dry,
the creaming of the skin
the oils, the ointments

the gauze, the woven layer,
the fine weave made from seaweed
that is so costly,
the skilled hands touching, smoothing
– something sacramental in that –
the practised re-bandaging,
the sense of wholeness
that comes from openness confined

the final trust
in the flesh's own healing essence,
as if it one day
could cast off its pharaoh's parcelling
to live again

hand dryers

like some friends
they need you to keep close:
move off
even an inch
and they will stop spraying warmth

some wheeze into life
as if bestowing their last gasp on you

some are inert, resisting
even the laying-on of palms

some emit a fierce heathrow roar,
a fearsome, searing burnt breath
worthy of a dragon

a few toy with you,
stopping, stuttering,
starting
and generally farting about
before they wash their hands of you

hair

fleeced from all our family,
the strands lay
commingled on the floor,
mown like the locks of auschwitz
or the hair of the heroes of thermopylae

blonde and brown and not so brown,
the hair said nothing
of its origins in loving;
i swept it up and took it up in my fingers,
enough for any number of lockets
on bold victorian bosoms

the serried strands
hugged each other
like bodies in a plague pit,
impersonal
in their embarrassing embraces,
their separate beings blurred
but not merged,
still obstinately human

they crissed and kissed and crossed
and wove themselves into a sampler
of what we were and might have been

they sang of how life hangs from a hair
and how, when the fates flash their shears,
all sheep shall be untangled from goats:
shaggy or shorn, they shall be known

they sang of how truth,
depicted by us as bald,
once had long, lustrous tresses,
and how the dark hair of hiroshima

was blinded out in a blink;
they sang of warp and weft
but they were powerless
to weave a pilgrim a shirt of penitence

i flung them wholesale on the fire
where they flared
in one united brightness,
true at last,
and then were gone,
leaving a few ominous black twists

dispatches from todoland

'SO WHAT'S THE TODO STORY, THEN?'
– NEWSPAPER EXECUTIVE, ON SEEING
'TO DO' SCRAWLED ON PART OF A PAGE PLAN

in the land of todo
gardens groan and overgrow,
beans go green,
turn stringy and straggly,
while plants get potbound in rows

brown's grounds
keep their capabilities,
hairdressers hover
with half-open scissors,
meals retain their savour
and no task sours

virgins wait, lips parted,
for a transit to the next kingdom,
where beauty sleeps

todo welcomes would-be drivers

yes, todo, gateway to nowhere,
a hinterland
of blocked plumbing,
teetering avalanches,
unread books, unwritten poems,
half-plastered alcoves,
where trains and babies
are always expected

where cavafy meets oblomov
clasping hands with gaudi
on the ithaca trail

tell yourself
over your cooling coffee
there is no disgrace
in being a denizen of todoland;
hope is ever-blooming here
but beware:
once you are done with it,
there is no return

crematorium cat

intent on mayhem,
the cat slinks
low-slung to the ground

a bird half in funeral garb,
half in sporting white
is in her sights

good day, sir magpie!
just one for sorrow

such rude life is a rebuke
to the artificial flowers
in uniform vases

could there be a killing
amid the detritus of death?

desolation already rules
among messages that read
as if selected or suggested
from an undertaker's list

much loved,
sadly missed,
always in our hearts

but always is a long time
and anyway
the cat is careless
of such consolations

the snake in the net

we knew there was one about
because
our neighbour told us with pride
of seeing one:
a grass snake, lovely, about this long,
the gesture said it all

but no thought prepared us
for the tableau at our pond:
in the net spread above heedless fish
to avert the heron,
he had caught himself:
rather than draw back,
he had forged forward,
getting more and more enmeshed

we had to cut him loose,
regardless of net strands;
but the long, lissom body,
its markings mimicking the net,
was lifeless

our guest from fabergé's workshop
would snaffle no more frogs;
our toads were safer
but our hearts were heavier

key question

aunt flora's keys
on rings and frayed strings,
on tags with faded labelling,
promise hours of discovery

rusty but intriguing,
whether short and stubby
or slim-wrought and ornate,
unfolding visions of tallboys,
of sideboards and secretaries

the only lack is ... a lock,
a door or drawer
to drag open and behold
aunt flora's forgotten gains

the house
where all these keys once hung
has been pillaged;
cash has changed hands
with more rustling than jingling

the clocks have gone quietly,
the armchairs without a groan;
cupboards, cabinets
have been crated or cremated;
the china cats and bunnies
like the presents from southend
have been released
from their glass-fronted hutch;
the flying ducks have migrated

and aunt flora
has been packed lovingly
in a case without a hinge
or a lock
or, for that matter, a key

the last indignity

death is a dullness

the pebble pilfered from the sea
dries to a dreadful dreariness;
the fish hauled flapping
from the confiding water
assumes an everyday tinge,
its metal tarnished:
its eye dulls to the conventional

the pheasant flattened by gunfire
is no more a king, he is dimmed,
limply bedraggled;
by the roadside, the cat
once pulsing with puss-purring life
seems dun, damp, drained

voices deaden in the face of death
as mourners maunder and meander
in muted tones;
music has to be cajoled
out of the lifeless air,
its measures draped in awe

as the deacon drones,
his funereal phrases falter
under a pall of ennui;
the drab earth
awaits its guest

at twelve today

they said that at twelve today
the cortège would pass

but i could not hear
the mourners' tread
for the disputes over who
should have the better view

they said that at twelve today
the workers would march

but i could not hear
their songs or slogans
for the sounds of police
demonstrating against peace

they said that at twelve today
the minister would speak

but i could not hear
his oil-fed phrases
for the armourers' chaff
about how to blow a man in half

cranmer's vigil

why play the man?
why, when the flames mount
and you begin to boil in your own sweat,
not shriek what first flies to your mind?

the sin, latimer, is not in confessing
but in having nothing to confess

poor master ridley!
condemned to be consumed piecemeal,
denied his last avowal of his firm flesh
and branded, not by the fire merely,
but by the scorching of scorn

a book burns as quickly as a man;
the pages turn idly
beneath the flamy fingers;
if any eye scans, it is impartial,
committed only to destruction

cry then, master ridley:
cry that virtue chars as black as sin
- and sometimes the phoenix flutters
from ashes of a better bird

for primo levi

why have good men died
and why do good men still die
before their moment?
i know the bad will also come
to an end, if not a bad end,
but what devours me
is the bland way they meld
into the indifferent

i face this one,
grab him by his metaphysicals,
his metaphorical beard,
his mythic balls,
i bawl into his face,
i look into his metaphorical pupils,
my gaze is rebuffed

he looks frustratingly the same
as before
and as he will again
when i am gone

a kelly doll of evil

you were more of a man
than those who sought to deny
your manhood;
when you too are vanished
and they are all vanquished
who knew the good from the bad
(never mind the truth)
and could not say
the unsayable
for fear it would be found
unhearable

someone with wrinkled brow
will still be saying
we must love one another, or die

while the undead
and the deniers
laugh at the very concept
of being unloved

joanne

i love joanne
... the legend is cut deep
and dauntlessly,
if a little crazily,
into the scuffed carriage door

for their carver
those three words were enough;
they should suffice
for me – but I find myself
impatient to know the end

was his labour justified,
the crouching gouging
in a treacherous train?
was joanne herself sitting
with lips moist and slightly parted
in pride,
as his crude knife
engraved her immortality?

or was his a bitter cut,
a deed more of defiance
than of expectation?

was his inscription
already monumental,
a crooked mockery
of journeys without joanne?

a happy man

you look like a happy man, i said,
as we swayed on the train;
i have to be, he replied,
who else
is going to be happy for me?
then he was gone,
a smiling black man with wispy beard
cast loose in the city

my mind cut back to johannesburg
and another black man
beaten up for grinning:
to the whites who walloped him,
it signified being cheeky,
their lordly due
was a downcast, cowed look

did my friend from the train
remain happy all day,
i wondered?
i could always try
being happy for him
but would he ever know?

the hanged man

the feet are first noticed,
a cliché, toes-down dangling
to tread on tiptoe on the air

the arms harmless,
the whole mobile
turning
in doleful pirouettes,
uncertain which of the wind's whims
to obey

the head cocked expectantly,
the face fixed in mock-gothic shock
at what could never be expected

cut down, he splays out all ways
like a lost glove
on a winter pavement

yet all is green,
it is the garden that startles
and the grass he lies on;
the willow trails her first buds
in the breeze
as if to tease his already-icing eyes
with spring

ukrainian spring

not yet april, and lilacs
can surely not be bred
out of this dead land

the cruel month is march
when early fruits,
very similar to men, women
and even children,
lie under blasted trees

they say poppies bloomed
above the shell craters of france;
but can these frozen bones,
picked over by dogs,
inspire anything new?

it is the noise, not birdsong
on this insane,
incessant guy fawkes night,
but brash whines and bangs
of all the doors to hell,
mind-blinding flashes
like flowers of abomination,
that those who stagger
from bolt-holes and burrows
will remember

address book

you do not cross them out,
the dead,
you forbear to tear off
their scuffed, corner-curled pages
or cancel those
who are missing, presumed gone:
the disappeared
who moved, or quarrelled
or simply dwindled
(is it that we lose touch
or that we lose
the habit of touching?)

you run your fingers over the names
as if printing them
in braille
on every sense,
yet they cannot fade:
even tippex
will leave a wraith-faint outline
to taunt you

in these phantom strings of figures,
these phones that ring-tring-trill
in echoey rooms,
these shades
of abandoned avenues, estranged streets,
are fragments of old friends,
figments of you

it is you
who hurt in all these houses,
you who haunt stairwells in flats
long since torn down

you walk on each and every street
seeking, straining
to descry indistinct impressions
of the dead and undead;
you quicken, then sickeningly slacken
as the thrill of recognition dies

pulled-at by hook-hands of the past
you turn the pages

more names mock you:
despite the laid-out lines of plenty,
it seems whole screeds of your life
are squared off
into brown departmental pigeon holes,
forwarding addresses,
wrong numbers, letters lost

studland bay

leaf rustle, wind kiss, cloud scurry,
a crowd of impressions
where sea and sky
celebrate white and blue

a heavy swell is running
as if the earth were shrugging
and water pouring off its shoulders,
or as if some guilty sea creature
were agitating
unsuspectable depths

too brilliant, this blue;
all seems well, and yet
it will take only the slightest shake
to unsettle nature's pact
with herself

out there are ships,
lives criss-crossing, rarely coalescing,
causing their own share
in the water's perturbation

up at the churchyard,
where leaning tombstones
act out the clashes of doings and deaths,
no voyagers are stirring
even in the freshening breeze

we wait, not for a sign or a sail
but for a spell breaker

girl

toffee-brown girl
you tease my taste buds
with your caramel arms,
montelimar neck
and butterscotch-silky legs

i have a feeling
you are not all treacle-textured
– beneath your scant wrapping
i fancy you are minto-white

i would like to bite you
where the brown borders on the white
...and explore
more of your tongue-tickling flavours,
toffee-burnt gleaming girl

the fiddler's dream

through a shrill-blowing, ill-bowing flurry of notes
from strumpets with trumpets in fur-filthy coats,
tubercular pipers flutter-tonguing like vipers
and hoboes with oboes more doleful than goats,
he limps, with his air of peering through a fog,
his v-sign thumbstick
and his lick-your-arse allsorts of a dog

the traveller, with the brass neck of his kind,
toting a pisspot for a passport
and a bundle full of wind

my kind of party, he hisses,
tuning a rosin-stained fiddle
and ominously tightening his bow
as beelzebub's syllabub noxiously bubbles
and a jiggling gigolo with a big hallo
conducts a saint-saëns singsong
to a half-pissed harpist's curdled chords

just my kind of party, says the fiddler

as he strikes up a reel that is almost surreal
and the dancing begins, toe to toe, heel to heel,
a vile charivari that old stradivari
would never envision, in gut or in steel;
free-flowing poteen from the witches' shebeen
makes the revellers randy, the moon-maidens mean
and amid the cacophony, if you can quaff any,
feel the effect as it splatters your spleen

then when midnight has struck you can see little puck
fly to summons some rum 'uns from piles of black muck:

an airy-fuck, fairy-fuck orgy of fairy folk
jostling and wassailing and goosing with glee,
spaced out on the honeydew, sod all the money due,
twist like an adder and flip like a flea;
see the bums in the rigging, the farting, the frigging,
the tits in the trees and the teasing of knees,
the fantastical testicles free to the breeze,
pubic hair on the g-string, fetid air on the e-string
and f-holes full-filled with the sleaze of the quays:
the crotchety, quavery, old-fangled fakers,
the bitchers, the brokers, the pogo-stick makers,
the dick-flicking rentboys and high-kicking doxies,
the black-booted whores with perpetual poxes,
the coke-sniffing pixies, the pasty-faced ponces,
the pipe-smoking pimps and the nasty old nonces,
a nitpicking, box-ticking picnic of critics,
a table of cynics from nerve-jangled clinics,
directors of quangos dance tangos, fandangos,
gerrymandering tories pat pole-dancing houris,
account-diddling bankers kiss wankers with cankers
while masochist wimps cringe to whip-cracking spankers,
nude gnomes with huge hard-ons run riot in gardens
and fumble the nymphs in ha-has and gazebos
as struck-off physicians pop pills and placebos

the buggers, the muggers, the manic bush-huggers,
the sluggers off luggers, the seedy song-pluggers,
while mortal man slumbers, they all make their numbers,
their sambas and rumbas, with cocks like cucumbers
and thighs of a size that would turn a saint green

then they suddenly cease and a pool foul with grease
is all that is left of the scene or obscene
as the traveller departs, and the pipes cease to keen

in the square

in mid-phrase,
the fiddler rests his bow arm,
the music dies on the air

his hearers rise
and stand, sheepish,
unsure whether to weep or to applaud

around jan palach
in václav square
the fire breathes deeply

the old men
stand stiff and straight,
flicking their tongues
unblinking, like lizards

the audience files out,
a little shame-faced,
as if some rite has been forgotten

down tiananmen square
the tanks trundle,
their tracks heedless
of hard, soft or brittle surface

the old men lick thin lips
flecked with spittle,
their lined necks evoke lizards
and their tongues flames

behind hooded eyes
they think of death
and wish it on the young

three wise monkeys

to hear no evil
and be deaf
to mirth, merriment and music

to speak no evil
and be dumb
in the face
of passion's protestations

to see no evil
and be blind
to the jewel wasp's palette of hues

if this is wisdom,
the stupid and the vain
are sniggering at us

while the wise falter,
the ignorant rejoice
in sight and sound and voice

this is the verse

this is the verse
that i made

i did not make the words,
i did not make the letters

i did not fashion the lines

i did not mould them by touch
on the wheel my name implies

nor did i haul them kicking
out of some dank recess or well

no, i caught them with my thoughts
and held them in my thoughts
and nurtured them in my thoughts

i think
i did not even make the thoughts

but out of all these negations
grew something like a yes

the great writer

asked to tea to meet her
i found her neat, cool, contained
over the prim table,
her face carved cold as keaton
or rachmaninoff
out of mount rushmore
and quiet, as if grave-swaddled
in the valley of kings

the more she drew inward,
the more i prattled,
the more she sat,
silently sizing me up,
the more i wrapped her web
about me
with my floundering

stifled in a killing jar,
i felt pinned out,
my wings wasted, losing lustre,
attracting dust

worse, this lepidopterous demise
was of my own weaving

did i wind up
in one of her display cases?
or was i just a passing bug
on the way
to a more interesting insect?

two haiku

(i)

naked and sharing
the bathroom with a wasp,
i ponder life's caprice

(ii)

he drank to forget
and then he forgot why
he had started drinking

nocturnal

sometimes at night i think of those that are dead
and i feel as if my brittle heart will break;
i think of the words i willingly left unsaid
and of the visits i wilfully did not make

i think each link into being until a chain
of circumstance ties me into a kind of death;
i ponder those i shall never see again
and i wonder how i can still sustain my breath

but my life will linger until i touch the brink
and others will briefly note that i have gone;
while time, with blanched indifference to what we think,
will dust its hands over these chalk marks and pass on

Printed in Great Britain
by Amazon

26414941R00059